19 VARIETIES OF GAZELLE

19 VARIETIES of GAZELLE

POEMS OF THE MIDDLE EAST

BY

Naomi Shihab Nye

GREENWILLOW BOOKS
An Imprint of HarperCollins*Publishers*

Special thanks to Salwa Nashashibi,
Aziz Shihab, Michael Nye,
Mina Greenstein, and Hilary Zarycky

The text type is Weiss.

Frontispiece: Gazelle tile, Jerusalem Pottery, Via Dolorosa, Old City.

Library of Congress Cataloging-in-Publication Data
Nye, Naomi Shihab.
    19 varieties of gazelle : poems of the Middle East / by Naomi
Shihab Nye.
        p.   cm.
    "Greenwillow Books."
    ISBN 0-06-009765-5 (trade). ISBN 0-06-009766-3 (lib. bdg.)
    1. Middle East—Poetry.   I. Title: Nineteen varieties of gazelle.
II. Title.   PS3564.Y44 A613 2002   811'.54—dc21   2002000771

1 2 3 4 5 6 7 8 9 10   First Edition

Introduction   x

🌿 Section One   1

➳ Section Two   85

FLINN, ON THE BUS

Three hours after the buildings fell,
he took a seat beside me.
Fresh out of prison, after 24 months,
You're my first hello!
Going home to Mom,
a life he would make better this time,
how many times
he'd been swept along before,
to things he should never have . . .
drink and dope,
but now he'd take responsibility.
Lawyers had done him wrong
and women too. He thought
about revenge, now he was out.
But I'm in charge. I'll think
before I act. I don't ever
want to go there again.
Two wrongs don't make a right.
Somehow, in his mouth, that day,
it sounded new.
The light came through the window
on a gentle-eyed man in a
"Focus on the Game" T-shirt,
who had given up
assault with deadly weapons,
no more, no good!

A man who had not seen TV in weeks,
secluding in his cell so colleagues
wouldn't trip him up,
extend his stay.
Who had not heard the news.
We rolled through green Oklahoma,
the bus windows made all the trees look bent.
A trick of refraction—
Flinn looked at his free hands
more than the fields,
turned them over in his lap,
no snap judgments, no quick angers,
I'll stand back, look at what happens,
think calmly what my next step should be.
It was not hard to nod,
to wish him well. But could I tell
what had happened in the world
on his long-awaited day,
what twists of rage greater
than we could ever guess
had savaged skylines, thousands of lives?
I could not. He'd find out
soon enough. Flinn, take it easy.
Peace is rough.   ✍❤

September 11, 2001

We start out as little bits of disconnected dust.

No, we start out as birds. In a nest, if we're lucky. Being fed, being tended.

We have no idea how many other birds are in their own little nests on their own branches.

Then, so very soon, much too soon, we are toppling from nests, changing species, and we're not birds anymore, now we are some kind of energetic gazelle leaping toward the horizon with hope spinning inside us, propelling us. . . .

Where does it come from? We are not responsible. We did not invent the gazelle.

*

All my life I thought about the Middle East, wrote about it, wondered about it, lived in it, visited it, worried about it, loved it. We are blessed and doomed at the same time.

I was born in the United States, but my father stared back toward the Middle East whenever he stood outside. Our kitchen smelled like the Middle East—garlic and pine nuts sizzled in olive oil, fried eggplant, hot pita bread. My father dropped sprigs of mint into our pots of hot tea. He had been happy as a boy in the Old City of Jerusalem with his Palestinian and Greek and Jewish and Armenian neighbors. But after the sad days of 1948, when his family lost their home and everything they owned, he wanted to go away. One of the few foreign university students in Kansas in the 1950s, he was a regular customer at the local drugstore soda fountain in his new little town. "He always looked dreamy, preoccupied, like he could see things other people couldn't see," the druggist told me twenty-five years later. Well yes, I thought. That's what immigrants look like. They always have other worlds in their minds.

My father and my American mother invented new dishes using Middle Eastern ingredients. We were proud without knowing it. Travelers from the Middle East often sat in circles in our backyard sharing figs and peaches and speaking in Arabic. Arabic music played in our house. Our father told better folk stories than anyone else's father—he had a gentle wit and almost never got mad. So kids from the neighborhood would camp out on our screened-in back porch, and we would all beg my father to tell more funny stories. It was a rich world to be in that had nothing to do with money or politics.

I got into the habit of writing little things down from the very beginning—not because they were more interesting than anyone else's "little things," but just so I could think about them. When I finally met some other Arab American writers (I was in my twenties by then), we felt we had all been writing parts of a giant collective poem, using the same bouquet of treasured images (was there anyone among us who had never mentioned a fig?)

It always felt good to be rooted and connected, but there were those deeply sorrowful headlines in the background to carry around like sad weights: the brutal occupation of Palestine, the war in Lebanon, the tragedies in Syria, the oppression of women in too many places (my father used to say when I was a teenager, "Do you realize how lucky you are?" and of course I didn't), acts of terrorism, both against Arabs and by Arabs, the rise of fundamentalism, violence in Egypt, upsets and upheavals, and later the Gulf War . . . a series of endless troubles.

Arab Americans had the additional sadness of feeling the Middle East was rarely represented in a balanced way in the mainstream U.S. media. Many of us had Jewish friends who shared our sorrows about the ongoing conflicts between our people. Couldn't they work it out?

We always tried to remember the abundant humor and resilience and the love of family. We listened to the music, the glittering *oud* and the flute, and we savored the food. We wore intricately embroidered dresses and vests. We read the poems and held them close in our hearts. As years went on, we learned about groups like Seeds of Peace, dedicated to bringing teenagers together for dialogue and understanding. We knew about Neve Shalom/Wahat-al-Salaam, the village deliberately, exactly balanced between Arabs and Jews. We knew about the *Sesame Street* program designed for both Arab and Jewish children.

We held on tightly to every optimistic fragment of news, every promising thread. We learned how to sew, we learned how to mend.

*

September 11, 2001, was not the first hideous day ever in the world, but it was the worst one many Americans had ever lived. May we never see another like it. For people who love the Middle East and have an ongoing devotion to cross-cultural understanding, the day felt sickeningly tragic in more ways than one. A huge shadow had been cast across the lives of so many innocent people and an ancient culture's pride.

Through the immense grief in the wake of this disaster, we grasped on to details to stay afloat.

For some reason I kept remembering a gentle Egyptian basket-seller on the streets of Cairo, and an elegant Arab man, an expert on brocade in the Old City of Jerusalem, who gave us twice the amount of cloth we paid for.

I remembered simple Arabic village breakfasts, creamy *labneh* fresh from its cheesecloth with delicate sliced cucumbers and scatterings of thyme . . . and a restaurant-owner, Waleed, who would make free lentil soup for my son who loved it, though it wasn't on his menu at that time of year.

A haunting thought returned again and again: the Arabs have always been famous for their generosity.

Messages poured in like waterfalls, tidal floods of messages all over the country, from one country to another: *Are you okay?*

I kept thinking, as did millions of other people, what can we do? Writers, believers in words, could not give up words when the going got rough. I found myself, as millions did, turning to poetry. But many of us have always turned to poetry. Why should it be any surprise that people find solace in the most intimate literary genre? Poetry slows us down, cherishes small details. A large disaster erases those details. We need poetry for nourishment and for noticing, for the way language and imagery reach comfortably into experience, holding and connecting it more successfully than any news channel we could name.

Perhaps Arab Americans must say, twice as clearly as anyone else, that we deplore the unbelievable, senseless sorrow caused by people from the Middle East. The losses cannot be measured. They will reverberate in so many lives throughout the coming years.

But also we must remind others never to forget the innocent citizens of the Middle East who haven't committed any crime. The people who are living solid, considerate lives, often in difficult conditions—especially the children, who struggle to maintain their beautiful hope.

And the old ones, who have been through so much already. I think of my Palestinian grandmother who lived till she was 106. She used to tease us by saying she didn't want to die "till everyone she didn't like died first." We think she succeeded. The truth was, she was very popular. She did not read or write, but was famous for her fabulous stories and offbeat wit and wisdom. In her lexicon politics were boring, and fanaticism was ridiculous.

The only place beyond Palestine my grandmother ever traveled was to Mecca, by bus. She was proud to be called a Hajji, to wear white clothes after her pilgrimage. She always worked hard to get stains out of everyone's dresses, scrubbing them with a stone. I think she would consider the recent tragedies a terrible stain on her religion. She would weep. She wanted people to worship in whatever ways they felt comfortable. To respect one another, sit together around the fire cracking almonds and drinking tea, and never forget to laugh, no matter what horrible things they had been through. What wisdom did she know that all these men can't figure out?

After writing about her in essays, poems, picture books, and a novel, I had thought I could let her rest. She's been dead for eight years now. But since September 11, 2001, she has swarmed into my consciousness, poking my sleep, saying, "It's your job. Speak for me too. Say how much I hate it. Say this is not who we are."

I dedicate these poems of my life to the wise grandmothers and to the young readers in whom I have always placed my best faith. If grandmothers and children were in charge of the world, there would never be any wars. Peace, friends. Please don't stop believing.

Naomi Shihab Nye
December 2001
San Antonio, Texas

Section ne

THERE WAS the method of kneeling,
a fine method, if you lived in a country
where stones were smooth.
Women dreamed wistfully of
hidden corners where knee fit rock.
Their prayers, weathered rib bones,
small calcium words uttered in sequence,
as if this shedding of syllables could
fuse them to the sky.

There were men who had been shepherds so long
they walked like sheep.
Under the olive trees, they raised their arms—
Hear us! We have pain on earth!
We have so much pain there is no place to store it!
But the olives bobbed peacefully
in fragrant buckets of vinegar and thyme.
At night the men ate heartily, flat bread
   and white cheese,
and were happy in spite of the pain,
because there was also happiness.

Some prized the pilgrimage,
wrapping themselves in new white linen
to ride buses across miles of sand.
When they arrived at Mecca
they would circle the holy places,
on foot, many times,
they would bend to kiss the earth
and return, their lean faces housing mystery.

While for certain cousins and grandmothers
the pilgrimage occurred daily,
lugging water from the spring
or balancing baskets of grapes.

These were the ones present at births,
humming quietly to perspiring mothers.
The ones stitching intricate needlework into
    children's dresses,
forgetting how easily children soil clothes.

There were those who didn't care about praying.
The young ones. The ones who had
   been to America.
They told the old ones, *you are wasting your time.*

   Time? The old ones prayed for the young ones.
They prayed for Allah to mend their brains,
for the twig, the round moon,
to speak suddenly in a commanding tone.

And occasionally there would be one
who did none of this,
the old man Fowzi, for example,
who beat everyone at dominoes,
insisted he spoke with God as he spoke with goats,
and was famous for his laugh.

FOR OTHER fruits my father was indifferent.
He'd point at the cherry trees and say,
"See those? I wish they were figs."
In the evenings he sat by our beds
weaving folktales like vivid little scarves.
They always involved a figtree.
Even when it didn't fit, he'd stick it in.
Once Joha was walking down the road
and he saw a figtree.
Or, he tied his camel to a figtree and went to sleep.
Or, later when they caught and arrested him,
his pockets were full of figs.

At age six I ate a dried fig and shrugged.
"That's not what I'm talking about!" he said,
"I'm talking about a fig straight from the earth—
gift of Allah!—on a branch so heavy
it touches the ground.
I'm talking about picking the largest, fattest,
    sweetest fig
in the world and putting it in my mouth."
(Here he'd stop and close his eyes.)

Years passed, we lived in many houses,
none had figtrees.
We had lima beans, zucchini, parsley, beets.
"Plant one!" my mother said,
but my father never did.
He tended garden half-heartedly, forgot to water,
let the okra get too big.
"What a dreamer he is. Look how many
things he starts and doesn't finish."

The last time he moved, I had a phone call,
my father, in Arabic, chanting a song
I'd never heard. "What's that?"
He took me out to the new yard.
There, in the middle of Dallas, Texas,
a tree with the largest, fattest,
sweetest figs in the world.
"It's a figtree song!" he said,
plucking his fruits like ripe tokens,
emblems, assurance
of a world that was always his own.

HE SANG with abandon,
combing his black, black hair.
Each morning in the shower,
first in Arabic, rivery ripples
of song carrying him back
to his first beloved land,
then in English, where his repertoire
was short. *No kind at all!* we'd shout,
throwing ourselves into the brisk arc
of his cologne for a morning kiss.
But he gave us freedom to be fools
if we needed to, which we certainly
would later, which we all do now and then,
perhaps a father's greatest gift—
that blessing.

N THE evenings the women
walk to the spring,
my cousins balance huge buckets
on their heads.
They know all the stories of water
that comes through pipes:
their brothers are digging trenches,
laying down tile.
On the roof a silver tank
will cook the water in the sun.
They know there are countries
where men and women kiss in the streets,
where a man's hand on a woman's knee
does not mean an earthquake.

Still they take the buckets,
the fat fold of cloth that rests
on the head, and go to the spring,
trains of women in twos and threes,
greeting each other with murmur and hum,
a nod so slight the bucket barely tips.

Pages are turning, centuries of breeze.
These feet write history on the dirt road
and no one reads it, unless you are here
to read it, unless you are thirsty
and cup your hands where the women
tell you to hold them,
throwing your head back
for the long sweet draft.

They know I can't carry the bucket.
Still they offer it, grinning.
They eat sour peaches and laugh
at the way I look into things,
as if there were something waiting there
to be seen. 🌿

I HAVE lived in the room of stone
where voices become bones
buried under us long ago.
You could dig for years
uncovering the same sweet dust.

My hands dream crescent-shaped cakes,
trapped moons on a narrow veined earth.
All day I am studying my hands—giving them
    new things to hold.

Travel, I say. They become boats.
Go—the bird squirms to detach from the arm.
Across the courtyards, a radio rises up and explodes.

What is the history of Europe to us if we cannot
    choose our own husbands?
Yesterday my father met with the widower,
    the man with no hair.
How will I sleep with him, I who have never slept
    away from my mother?

Once I bought bread from the vendor with the
   humped back.
I carried it home singing,
the days had doors in them
that would swing open in front of me.

Now I copy the alphabets of three languages,
imagining the loops in my Arabic letters are eyes.
What you do when you are tired of what you see,

what happens to the gray body
when it is laid in the earth,
these are the subjects which concern me.
But they teach algebra.
They pull our hair back and examine our nails.

Every afternoon, predictable passage of sun
   across a wall.
I would fly out of here. Travel, I say.
I would go so far away my life would be
   a small thing behind me.

They teach physics, chemistry.
I throw my book out the window,
watch the pages scatter like wings.
I stitch the professor's jacket
to the back of his chair.

There is something else we were born for.
I almost remember it. While I write,
a ghost writes on the same tablet,
achieves a different sum.

for Sitti Khadra, north of Jerusalem

MY GRANDMOTHER'S hands recognize grapes,
the damp shine of a goat's new skin.
When I was sick they followed me,
I woke from the long fever to find them
covering my head like cool prayers.

My grandmother's days are made of bread,
a round pat-pat and the slow baking.
She waits by the oven watching a strange car
circle the streets. Maybe it holds her son,
lost to America. More often, tourists,
who kneel and weep at mysterious shrines.
She knows how often mail arrives,
how rarely there is a letter.
When one comes, she announces it, a miracle,
listening to it read again and again
in the dim evening light.

My grandmother's voice says
nothing can surprise her.
Take her the shotgun wound and the crippled baby.
She knows the spaces we travel through,

the messages we cannot send—our voices are short
and would get lost on the journey.
Farewell to the husband's coat,
the ones she has loved and nourished,
who fly from her like seeds into a deep sky.
They will plant themselves. We will all die.

My grandmother's eyes say Allah is everywhere,
    even in death.
When she speaks of the orchard
and the new olive press,
when she tells the stories of Joha
and his foolish wisdoms,
He is her first thought, what she really thinks of is
    His name.

"Answer, if you hear the words under the words—
otherwise it is just a world
with a lot of rough edges,
difficult to get through, and our pockets
full of stones." 🦋

TWO GIRLS danced, red flames winding.
I offered my shoes to the gypsies,
threw back my head, and yelled.

All day their hillocks of cheese
had been drying on a goat hide
stretched in the sun.
So it was true—they came in the night,
they set their dark tents flapping.
Gypsies see right through you,
I'd heard a man say in town.
But did they like what they saw?

To live without roads seemed one way
not to get lost. To make maps
of stone and grass, to rub stars together,
find a spark.

I gave American shoes, sandals from Greece.
They held each one curiously, shy to put them on.
Later the shoes disappeared into the tent
and I walked home with their drums in my belly.
Maybe they would use them as vases,
drawers. At least there were choices,
not like a sword, which did only one thing,
or a house, which sat and sat in the desert
after the goats and music had blown away.

SO YOU come with these maps in your head
and I come with voices chiding me to
"speak for my people"
and we march around like guardians of memory
till we find the man on the short stool
who makes brooms.

Thumb over thumb, straw over straw,
he will not look at us.
In his stony corner there is barely room
for baskets and thread,
much less the weight of our faces
staring at him from the street.
What he has lost or not lost is his secret.

You say he is like all the men,
the man who sells pistachios,
the man who rolls the rugs.
Older now, you find holiness in anything
that continues, dream after dream.
I say he is like nobody,
the pink seam he weaves
across the flat golden face of this broom
is its own shrine, and forget about the tears.

In the village the uncles will raise their *kefiyahs*
from dominoes to say, no brooms in America?
And the girls who stoop to sweep the courtyard
will stop for a moment and cock their heads.
It is a little song, this thumb over thumb,
but sometimes when you wait years
for the air to break open
and sense to fall out,
it may be the only one.

Jerusalem

E HAD also lived in Spain
so we stood under a glossy loquat tree
telling of *madres y milagros*
with clumsy tongues.
It seemed strange in the mouth
of this Arab, but no more so
than everything.
Across his valley the military
settlement gleamed white.
He said, That's where the guns live,
as simply as saying, It needs sun,
a plant needs sun.
He stooped to unsheathe an eggplant
from its nest of leaves,
purple shining globe,
and pressed it on me.
I said No, no, I don't want
to take things before they are ripe,
but it was started already,
handfuls of marble-sized peaches,
hard green *mish-mish* and delicate lilt
of beans. Each pocket swelled
as he breathed mint leaves,
bit the jagged edge.

He said every morning found him here,
before the water boiled on the flame
he came out to this garden,
dug hands into earth saying, *I know you*
and earth crumbled rich layers
and this result of their knowing—
a hillside in which no inch went unsung.
His enormous onions held light
and the trees so weighted with fruits
he tied the branches up.

And he called it *querido, corazon,*
all the words of any language
connecting to the deep place
of darkness and seed. He called it
ya habibi in Arabic, my darling tomato,
and it called him governor, king,
and some days he wore no shoes.

West Bank

"He only listened to his own secret bell, ringing,
and saw another winter come."
—Mahmoud Darwish

WHAT WATER she poured on the floor
was more than was needed. Someone suggested
she mop in strips as they did
on the television, yet her buckets were full,
the great buckets of field and orchard,
she was dragging them room to room
in a house that already looked clean.

The tune she hummed was nobody's tongue.
Already she had seen the brothers go off
in airplanes, she did not like the sound.
Skies opened and took people in.
The tune was long and had one line.

And the soldiers flipping ID cards,
the men who editorialized blood
till it was pale and not worth spilling,
meant nothing to her.
She was a woman shopping for fabric.
She was walking with her neck straight,
her eyes placed ahead.
What oil she rubbed on the scalp was pure.
The children she spoke to were news,
were listening, had names
and a scraped place on the elbow.
She could place a child in a bucket
and bathe it, could stitch the mouth
in the red shirt closed.

ACH TIME you go through this
you lose a little less color

the water is less
pink, blue, or gray

this is what i try to say:
don't let them wring it out of you

because they like starch,
don't let that apply to your neck

you are real, 100% cotton,
you can wrinkle, accept that as a gift

and accept these rinses,
they are tedious

they will come
again and again

after awhile, you will have
nothing more they can take

1.

UNCLE MOHAMMED, you mystery, you distant
    secretive face,
lately you travel across the ocean and tap me
    on my shoulder
and say "See?" And I think I know what you are
    talking about,
though we have never talked, though you have
    never traveled anywhere
in twenty-five years, or anywhere anyone
    knows about.
Since my childhood, you were the one I cared for,
you of all the uncles, the elder brother
    of the family.
I'd pump my father, "But why did he go
    to the mountain?
What happened to him?" and my father, in his
    usual quiet way,
would shrug and say, "Who knows?"
All I knew was you packed up, you moved
    to the mountain,
you would not come down.

This fascinated me: How does he get food?
    Who does he talk to?
What does he do all day?
In grade school my friends had uncles who rode
    motorcycles,
who cooked steaks outdoors or paid for movies.
I preferred you, in all your silence.
In my mind you were like a god, living close
    to clouds,
fearless and strong, with no one to sing you
    to sleep.
And I wanted to know you, to touch hands,
    to have you look at me
and recognize your blood, a small offspring
who did not find you in the least bit
nuts.

2.

I wonder how much news you know. That Naomi,
    your sister
for whom I was partially named, is dead.

That one brother shot himself "by mistake"—
that your brothers Izzat and Mufli have twenty-two
children already marrying each other.
That my father edits one of the largest newspapers
    in America
but keeps an Arabic inscription above his door,
    Ahlan Wa Sahlan,
a door you will never enter.

We came to your country, Uncle, we lived there
    a year
among sheep and stones, camels and fragrant oils,
and you would not come down to see us.
I think that hurt my father, though he never said so.
It hurt me, scanning the mountains
    for sight of your hut,
quizzing the relatives and learning nothing.
Are you angry with us? Do you think my father
    forgot you
when he packed his satchel and boarded the ship?

Believe me, Uncle, my father is closer to you
than you know. When he tends plants,
he walks slowly. His steps sing of the hills.
And when he stirs the thick coffee and grinds
    the cardamom seed
you think he feels like an American?
You think he forgets the call to prayer?

Oh Uncle, forgive me, how long is your beard?

3.

Maybe you had other reasons.
Maybe you didn't go up the mountain
because you were angry.
This is what I am learning, the voice I hear
when I wake at 3 a.m.
It says, Teach me how little I need to live
and I can't tell if it is me talking, or you,
or the walls of the room. How little, how little,
and the world jokes and says, how much.

Money, events, ambitions, plans, oh Uncle,
I have made myself a quiet place in the swirl.
I think you would like it.
Yesterday I learned how many shavings of wood
    the knife discards
to leave one smoothly whittled spoon.
Today I read angles of light through the window,
first they touch the floor, then the bed,
till everything is luminous, curtains flung wide.
As for friends, they are fewer and dearer,
and the ones who remain seem also to be
    climbing mountains
in various ways, though we dream we will meet
    at the top.
Will you be there?
Gazing out over valleys and olive orchards,
telling us sit, sit,
you expected us all along.

KNOW who's in there

girl spinning string around her finger

boy with a bruised eye

If he lifts his other eye to the sun
his father rises saying, "Wait, wait"
but this fruit is too slow

The pit of this peach
breaks a hundred teeth

*

In suits the color of olive trees
soldiers stand and stand

but not as olive trees stand
at the gate to the camp

They think they see both ways

They look past the widow with a hand
on her daughter's shoulder

the schoolgirl's pleated skirt

watching for something bigger
or worse

*

In the next town
a man sets tea on our table

He does not speak
He glides from the kitchen

a pot of steaming water
a pot of steaming milk

His brother has been beaten by soldiers
He saw the blood come out of the nose

Because of this he is walking
very slowly so not one drop

exceeds its edge

*

Yesterday the soldiers smashed
Lena's sink and tub and tiles

They whipped a father in front of his sons
ages 2 and 4

They do this all the time
The house filled with water

They locked the door on the crying boys
taking the father

Believe me Lena says
They had no reason

On the steps of the National Palace Hotel
soldiers peel oranges

throwing back their heads so the juice
runs down their throats

This must be their coffee break
guns slung sideways

They are laughing
stripping lustily

They know what sweetness lives within
How can they know this and forget

so many other things?

*

The olive's dusky gray-green shadow
won't leave a single one of its people alone

It follows them inside their own shadows
It loves them when they think there is no more
    loving

A man places his hand into the river
that holds him back

His dream crosses the slim water
What happens to the man and dream who get

separated?

Some people place their whole bodies
inside a dream
A woman steps out of a dream
with fresh almonds wrapped in a towel

holding them out
to any open mouth

for Palestine

WHEN YOU lunch in a town
which has recently known war
under a calm slate sky mirroring none of it,
certain words feel impossible in the mouth.
Casualty: too casual, it must be changed.
A short man stacks mounds of pita bread
on each end of the table, muttering
something about more to come.
Plump birds landing on park benches
surely had their eyes closed recently,
must have seen nothing of weapons or blockades.
When the woman across from you whispers
I don't think we can take it anymore
and you say there are people praying for her
in the mountains of Himalaya and she says
Lady, it is not enough, then what?

A plate of *hummus*, dish of tomato,
friends dipping bread—
I will not marry till there is true love, says one,
throwing back her cascade of perfumed hair.
He says the University of Texas seems
    remote to him
as Mars, and last month he stayed in his house
for 26 days. He will not leave, he refuses to leave.
In the market they are selling
men's shoes with air vents, a beggar displays
the giant scab of leg he must drag
    from alley to alley,
and students argue about
the best ways to protest.

In summers, this cafe is full.
Today only our table sends laughter into the trees.
What cannot be answered checkers the tablecloth
between the squares of white and red.
Where do the souls of hills hide
when there is shooting in the valleys?

What makes a man with a gun seem bigger
than a man with almonds? How can there be war
and the next day eating, a man stacking plates
on the curl of his arm, a table of people
toasting one another in languages of grace:
For you who came so far;
For you who held out, wearing a black scarf
to signify grief;
For you who believe true love can find you
amidst this atlas of tears linking one town
to its own memory of mortar,
when it was still a dream to be built
and people moved here, believing,
and someone with sky and birds in his heart
said this would be a good place for a park. 🍃

IT WAS never too strong for us:
make it blacker, Papa,
thick in the bottom,
tell again how years will gather
in small white cups,
how luck lives in a spot of grounds.

Leaning over the stove, he let it
boil to the top, and down again.
Two times. No sugar in his pot.
And the place where men and women
break off from one another
was not present in that room.
The hundred disappointments,
fire swallowing olive-wood beads
at the warehouse, and the dreams
tucked like pocket handkerchiefs
into each day, took their places
on the table, near the half-empty
dish of corn. And none was
more important than the others,
and all were guests. When
he carried the tray into the room,
high and balanced in his hands,
it was an offering to all of them,

stay, be seated, follow the talk
wherever it goes. The coffee was
the center of the flower.
Like clothes on a line saying
You will live long enough to wear me,
a motion of faith. There is this,
and there is more. 🦋

THE ARABS used to say,
When a stranger appears at your door,
feed him for three days
before asking who he is,
where he's come from,
where he's headed.
That way, he'll have strength
enough to answer.
Or, by then you'll be
such good friends
you don't care.

Let's go back to that.
Rice? Pine nuts?
Here, take the red brocade pillow.
My child will serve water
to your horse.

No, I was not busy when you came!
I was not preparing to be busy.
That's the armor everyone put on
to pretend they had a purpose
in the world.

I refuse to be claimed.
Your plate is waiting.
We will snip fresh mint
into your tea.

MAN letters the sign for his grocery
in Arabic and English.
Paint dries more quickly in English.
The thick swoops and curls of Arabic letters
stay moist and glistening
till tomorrow when the children
show up jingling their dimes.

They have learned the currency of the New World,
carrying wishes for gum and candies
shaped like fish.
They float through the streets,
diving deep to the bottom,
nosing rich layers of crusted shell.

One of these children will tell a story
that keeps her people alive.
We don't know yet which one she is.
Girl in the red sweater dangling a book bag,
sister with eyes pinned to the barrel
of pumpkin seeds.
They are lettering the sidewalk with their steps.

They are separate and together and a little bit late.
Carrying a creased note, "Don't forget."
Who wrote it? They've already forgotten.
A purple fish sticks to the back of the throat.
Their long laughs are boats they will ride and ride,
making the shadows that cross each other's smiles.

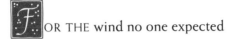OR THE wind no one expected

For the boy who does not know the answer

For the graceful handle I found in a field
attached to nothing
pray it is universally applicable

For our tracks which disappear
the moment we leave them

For the face peering through the cafe window
as we sip our soup

For cheerful American classrooms sparkling
with crisp colored alphabets
happy cat posters
the cage of the guinea pig
the dog with division flying out of his tail
and the classrooms of our cousins
on the other side of the earth
how solemn they are
how gray or green or plain
how there is nothing dangling
nothing striped or polka-dotted or cheery

no self-portraits or visions of cupids
and in these rooms the students raise their hands
and learn the stories of the world

For library books in alphabetical order
and family businesses that failed
and the house with the boarded windows
and the gap in the middle of a sentence
and the envelope we keep mailing ourselves

For every hopeful morning given and given
and every future rough edge
and every afternoon
turning over in its sleep

PALESTINIAN GIRLS with huge dark moons
under their eyes stand in line seven hours
for seven pieces of bread.
WATCHING AND WAITING, the caption says.
I can't feed them. Though I reach out
the hands of my hands of my hands.

On the desk, a gold camel sleeps in a bowl.
I put it there. It hasn't left.
Tell the story of a boy who sleeps
under the wall of a broken house
counting his fingers.
After so many dead people
they don't scare him anymore.
"Get up. If I can do it you can do it."
So he won't fall into the hole nobody
climbs out of. The well that swallows
buckets till the woman squeezes water
from the hem of her dress.

Tell me how to live so many lives at once.

Did you ever see a bee's little bucket?
I was 39 before I saw. Dipping into flowers,
the bee holds the bucket with its feet,
filling it, flying home pollen-rich,
and if someone puts a screen at the mouth
of the hive, the bucket catches when
the bee flies in. It has a handle.

Where does it get the bucket?
It spins it from its own body.
Why are bees so lucky?

And the boy in my house stoops
to the ground, gathering clipped grass,
piling mountains on the sidewalk,
light draining quietly from the street.
Saying "Stop," saying "Watch,"
and I want to, because in this world
there is nothing better to do.

"I dreamed I was 6 years old,
6 feet 10 inches tall, and I had to change
all the lightbulbs. If you think
about something before you go to sleep,
does that mean you can dream it?
I'll think about you."

You and you and you.
Mr. Laguna, who floats on his porch
inside a sweet blur of leaf . . .
for a year he begged to come home,
even on a walker,
even with no more hairs on his head.
He wanted the sunlight that rolls
everything together.
He wanted to give you a rabbit
in plaid pants.
Pick my cilantro, he says,
calling you The Baby.

He doesn't see you growing bigger
than all of us, looming over our street
like the white tower that says PIONEER
at the mill. They take wheat
and grind it into flour
for cinnamon biscuit, waffle, bread.
The men go home with flour in their cuffs.

This year, next year.
In Honolulu you learn to say,
"I am not sorry" in Hawaiian.
You tack it to the wall
where it soaks into my eyes,
day after windy day,
as students congregate,
as news filters toward us
through the big sky. I would like
to be even farther away,
I would like not to agree.

We are not sorry.
We are not sorry.
We can't be sorry enough.

LOOSE IN his lap, the hands.
And always a necktie,
as some worlds are made complete
by single things.
Graveled voice,
bucket raised on old ropes.
You know how a man can get up,
get dressed, and think
the world is waiting for him?
At night darkness knits
a giant cap to hold the dreams in.
A wardrobe of neckties with slanted stripes.
Outside oranges are sleeping, eggplants,
fields of wild sage. An order
from the government said,
You will no longer pick this sage
that flavors your whole life.
And all the hands smiled.
Tonight the breathing air carries
headlines that will cross the ocean
by tomorrow. Bar the door.

HEN WORD of his death arrived
we sat in a circle for days
crying or not crying

long ago in the other country
girls balanced buckets
on their heads

now the old sweet water
rose from the spring
to swallow us

brothers shrank
children grew old
it felt fine to say nothing
about him
or something small

the way he carried
oranges and *falafel*
in his pockets

the way he was always
slightly mad

what he said to each
the last time
we saw him
hurt the worst

those unwritten letters
banging each head
till it felt bruised

now he would stand at the mirror
knotting his tie
for the rest of so many lives

LITTLE SISTER Ibtisam,
our sleep flounders, our sleep tugs
the cord of your name.
Dead at 13, for staring through
the window into a gun barrel
which did not know you wanted to be
a doctor.

I would smooth your life in my hands,
pull you back. Had I stayed in your land,
I might have been dead too,
for something simple like staring
or shouting what was true
and getting kicked out of school.
I wandered stony afternoons
owning all their vastness.

Now I would give them to you,
guiltily, you, not me.
Throwing this ragged grief into the street,
scissoring news stories free from the page
but they live on my desk with letters, not cries.

How do we carry the endless surprise
of all our deaths? Becoming doctors
for one another, Arab, Jew,
instead of guarding tumors of pain
as if they hold us upright?

People in other countries speak easily
of being early, late.
Some will live to be eighty.
Some who never saw it
will not forget your face.

"To feel the love of people whom we love is a fire that feeds our
life. But to feel the affection that comes from those whom we
do not know . . . is something still greater and more beautiful . . ."
—Pablo Neruda

1.

BECAUSE OUR country has entered
into war, we can have
no pleasant pauses anymore—

instead, the nervous turning
one side to another,
each corner crowded by the far
but utterly particular
voices of the dead,

trees, fish, children,
calling, calling,
wearing the colorful plastic shoes
so beloved in the Middle East,
bleeding from the skull,
the sweet hollow along the neck.

I forget why. It's been changed.
For whatever it was

we will crush the vendor
who stacked sesame rings
on a tray
inside the steady gaze
of stones.
He will lose his balance
after years of perfect balance.

Catch him! Inside every sleep
he keeps falling.

2.

I support all people on earth
who have bodies like and unlike my body,
skins and moles and old scars,
secret and public hair,
crooked toes. I support
those who have done nothing large,
sifter of lentils, sifter of wisdoms,
speak. If we have killed no one
in the name of anything bad or good,
may light feed our leafiest veins.

I support clothes in the wash-kettle,
a woman stirring and stirring

with stick, paddle, soaking out grime,
simple clothes the size of bodies
pinned to the sky.

3.

What we learned left us.
None of it held.

Now the words ignite.
Slogans knot around necks
till faces bulge.

Windows of sand, doorways,
sense of shifting
each time you blink—

that dune? Used to be
a house. And the desert
soaking up echoes—

those whom we did not know
think they know us now.

Welcome to Abu Dhabi,
the Minister of Culture said.
You may hold my falcon as we visit.
He slipped a leather band around my arm
and urged the bird to step on board.
It wore a shapely leather hood.
Or otherwise, the host described,
the bird might pluck your very eyes.
My very eyes were blinking hard
behind the glasses that they wore.
The falcon's claws, so hooked and huge,
gripped firmly on the leather band.
I had to hold my arm out high.
My hand went numb. The heavens shone
a giant gold beyond our room.
I had no memory why I'd come
to see this man.
A falcon dives, and rips, and kills!
I think he likes you though.
It was the most I could have hoped for then.
We mentioned art.
We drank some tea.
He offered to remove the hood.
I said the bird looked very good just wearing it.
All right by me. 🦋

ONCE SINGING would rise
in sweet sirens over the hills
and even if you were working
with your trees or books
or cooking something simple
for your own family,
you washed your hands,
combed water through your hair.

Mountains of rice, shiny shoes,
a hurricane of dancing.
Children wearing little suitcoats
and velvet dresses fell asleep in circles
after eating 47 Jordan almonds.

*Who's getting married? Who's come home
from the far place over the seas?*

Sometimes you didn't even know.
You ate all that food without knowing.
Kissed both cheeks of anybody who passed,
slapping the drum, reddening your palm.
Later you were full, rich,
with a party in your skin.

Where does fighting
come into this story?

Fighting got lost from somewhere else.
It is not what we like: to eat, to drink, *to fight*.

Now when the students gather quietly
inside their own classroom
to celebrate the last day of school,
the door to the building
gets blasted off.
Empty chairs where laughter used to sit.
Laughter lived here
jingling its pocket of thin coins
and now it is hiding.

It will not come to the door dressed as a soapseller,
a peddler of matches, the old Italian
from the factory in Nablus
with his magic sack of sticks.

They have told us we are not here
when we were always here.
Their eraser does not work.

See the hand-tinted photos of young men:
too perfect, too still.
The bombs break everyone's
sentences in half.
Who made them? Do you know anyone
who makes them? The ancient taxi driver
shakes his head back and forth
from Jerusalem to Jericho.
They will not see, he says slowly,
the story behind the story,
they are always looking for the story after the story
which means they will never understand the story.

Which means it will go on and on.

How can we stand it if it goes on and on?
It is too long already.
No one even gets a small bent postcard
from the far place over the seas anymore.

No one hears the soldiers come at night
to pluck the olive tree from its cool sleep.

Ripping up roots. This is not a headline
in your country or mine.
No one hears the tiny sobbing
of the velvet in the drawer.

TIP THEIR mouths open to the sky.
Turquoise, amber,
the deep green with fluted handle,
pitcher the size of two thumbs,
tiny lip and graceful waist.

Here we place the smallest flower
which could have lived invisibly
in loose soil beside the road,
sprig of succulent rosemary,
bowing mint.

They grow deeper in the center of the table.

Here we entrust the small life,
thread, fragment, breath.
And it bends. It waits all day.
As the bread cools and the children
open their gray copybooks
to shape the letter that looks like
a chimney rising out of a house.

And what do the headlines say?

Nothing of the smaller petal
perfectly arranged inside the larger petal
or the way tinted glass filters light.
Men and boys, praying when they died,
fall out of their skins.
The whole alphabet of living,
heads and tails of words,
sentences, the way they said,
"Ya'Allah!" when astonished,
or "ya'ani" for "I mean"—
a crushed glass under the feet
still shines.
But the child of Hebron sleeps
with the thud of her brothers falling
and the long sorrow of the color red.

1.

I BREAK this toast for the ghost
   of bread in Lebanon.
The split stone, the toppled doorway.

Someone's kettle has been crushed.
Someone's sister has a gash
   above her right eye.

And now our tea has trouble being sweet.
A strawberry softens, turns musty,

overnight each apple grows a bruise.
I tie both shoes on Lebanon's feet.

All day the sky in Texas that has seen
   no rain since June
is raining Lebanese mountains, Lebanese trees.

What if the air grew damp with
   the names of mothers?
The clear-belled voices of first graders

pinned to the map of Lebanon like a shield?
When I visited the camp of the opposition

near the lonely Golan, looking northward toward
Syria and Lebanon, a vine was springing pinkly
    from a tin can

and a woman with generous hips like my mother's
said, "Follow me."

2.

Someone was there. Someone not there now
was standing. In the wrong place
with a small moon-shaped scar on his cheek
and a boy by the hand.
Who had just drunk water, sharing the glass.
Not thinking about it deeply
though they might have, had they known.
Someone grown and someone not-grown.
Who imagined they had different amounts
    of time left.

This guessing-game ends with our hands in the air,
becoming air.
One who was there is not there, for no reason.
Two who were there.

It was almost too big to see.

3.

Our friend from Turkey says language is so delicate
he likens it to a darling.

We will take this word in our arms.
It will be small and breathing.
We will not wish to scare it.
Pressing lips to the edge of each syllable.
Nothing else will save us now.

ECAUSE THE eye has a short shadow or
it is hard to see over heads in the crowd?

If everyone else seems smarter
but you need your own secret?

If mystery was never your friend?

If one way could satisfy
the infinite heart of the heavens?

If you liked the king on his golden throne
more than the villagers carrying
baskets of lemons?

If you wanted to be sure
his guards would admit you to the party?

> The boy with the broken pencil
> scrapes his little knife against the lead
> turning and turning it as a point
> emerges from the wood again

> If he would believe his life is like that
> he would not follow his father into war

T IS possible we will not meet again
on earth. To think this fills my throat
with dust. Then there is only the sky
tying the universe together.

Just now the neighbor's horse must be standing
patiently, hoof on stone, waiting for his day
to open. What you think of him,
and the village's one heroic cow,
is the knowledge I wish to gather.
I bow to your rugged feet,
the moth-eaten scarves that knot your hair.

Where we live in the world
is never one place. Our hearts,
those dogged mirrors, keep flashing us
moons before we are ready for them.
You and I on a roof at sunset,
our two languages adrift,
heart saying, Take this home with you,
never again,
and only memory making us rich.

1.

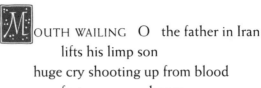

OUTH WAILING   O   the father in Iran
          lifts his limp son
     huge cry shooting up from blood
          feet   bones

so a woman across the earth   awakens startled
               at 4 a.m.
     she can't hear 50,000 together but she can
               hear him

     and her own son's finely-meshed breath
          as he tosses in his sheet
     dreaming of the glacier he poked
               with a stick
     even though   even though
          old blue ice   easing
          lower every year

Baba Kamalyari, 71, saw the earth tremble
        "like nature kicking the cradle.
I saw the mountain slide toward the village
and said, 'Allah Akbar, I am ready to die!'
        But I lived and all the younger ones
    were taken from me, all because of this rock."

2.

Once we read books that told what to eat,
        how to live,
    we snipped cheesecloth into circles
        for sprouting jars.

The Bach Flower Remedies indicated oak
"for depression suffered by brave people
who fight strongly against adverse conditions
        without losing hope."
We never had to try it. Or gorse, "for very
                great hopelessness."
Lelord Kordel said healthy Argentinians enjoy
            pan-fried steaks

with their eggs for breakfast, suggesting we
                try this "on occasion."
                But we didn't.
Better the watercress and whole grain chapati,
        the raspberry vinaigrette!

"Take care of yourself at every moment—of
        everything you say, do, think.
When there is vigilance, there is no fall."
And what did they eat in Iran? Hearty earthen
                meals, flat bread
        from round ovens, mint and rice . . .
                they ate until the earth ate them.

I feel ashamed for anything I ever explained.

ON ONE side of the world
he's fanning the fire he started
on the other side of the world.

From the sofa he names grandchildren,
the snow in his voice making little peaks
on the table in front of him.
You don't come to see me,
same leaf of mint crushed and crushed
in the fist. *I'm here all the time.*
His television blurs into one long connected story
steaming out of the set, sometimes with that clicker
in his hand he switches channels so fast
the news merges with the people who never stop
dancing and he clicks it off, mad.

He wants us to drink juice on top of tea.

I've sat with him behind the counter at work.
He fusses at a hundred dollar bill for diapers.
He shouts if they leave the cool drinks door
open two seconds. I've wanted
to follow them outside,
"He's not yelling at you. He's yelling at the soldiers
who filled in Abu Radhi's well with stones and dirt
back home. The ones who told him
to get lost, lost, lost.
He still argues with them every day. Please excuse."
I tell him, "Listen, there's a man at the library,
leaning into fiction, the back of his T-shirt says
PRAY FOR WIND."

"Honey I do. Believe me. Every single day."

Sometimes when I walk in the door
of his apartment,
bits of Kleenex stuck to the carpet
from all those kids,
I can't believe it hasn't blown away.

He says the news is all made up.
Between the place it happens
and the place it enters our ears, a hundred men
twist and turn their tiny tools,
making it different, giving it their own slant.
He says, "You, you, you don't even feed me meat
when I come to your house, what do you know?"

He's staring at the line where the wall
turns into a ceiling.
He's staring at the fine seam of plaster
and the haze of dust.
He's staring at the frayed hem along
the bottom of the couch.
He's not staring at the fringe
on his wife's golden scarf.
He's staring at the tea glass as if
it could speak from that
little sugared layer left in the bottom.

He's wearing a black suit and red tie
and starched white shirt
every day of his life because no one
will be able to see him
in his coffin except maybe the angels
and what do they care?
Not about suits. He's smiling a sad smile.

"Tell me about my father
and the one spot on his head
that hair would never grow from. Tell me
about the days of old Palestine."

"Your father? You know your father."

"Something he did as a boy
that I could never guess.
A fragment that's almost lost."

"It's all lost."

"It's not!"

He's staring at the longest arm of the plant that
    crawls up the wall.

"Your father . . ." he says. But doesn't
    mention him again.
"That world we lived in. I knew it by heart.
Every scent and every tree. I felt the fig
inside my skin. I could tell
when water boiled in the other room.

It was a great . . . sweetness. Sometimes I stood
    on the roof
looking out from our mountain across the valley
and the olive trees felt like parts of my own body.
I stretched out everywhere. I am sick
    for losing this."

And the day is long. The day has
    such empty places in it.

"If you start from a world like that,
the rest of your life you're looking for it.
Especially if you go somewhere else.
Did you see those old Greek men at the festival?
They know what I'm talking about.
And they still have Greece!
All these cars and apartment buildings
mean nothing to me.
You think they do? You think I care about my car?
You think I care about money? It never knows you.
My children came to the United States.
I care about my children."

Sometimes we talk as if we were sandpaper rubbing.

One of his sons skims past me at gatherings,
"I'll bet you don't know my name"
as if a hundred years ago I made him mad.

Cousins? Hundreds of cousins.
We wear the same glasses.
But they are handsome and slick their hair back.

They laugh easily. They have not fallen
into the lost well. Sometimes we watch our fathers
with the same quietness. We have an idea.
Where are we all going?
Into the next new world of the next new day.
What will happen?

We will always be waiting for them
    to tell us something.
See how restless they are getting? They will
    lift the blanket
draped over the foot of the bed to look under it.
They will be waiting, as people in exile
are always waiting,
for something, one thing, to fit again, that is bigger
than their own clothes.

IN THE corner of every Arab kitchen,
 an enormous plastic container
of olives is waiting for another meal.
 Green tight-skinned olives,
planets with slightly pointed ends—
 after breakfast, lunch, each plate
hosts a pyramid of pits in one corner.
 Hands cross in the center
of the table over the olive bowl.
 If any are left they go back to
the olive jar to soak again with sliced lemon and oil.
 Everyone says
it was a good year for the trees.

At the border an Israeli crossing-guard asked
 where I was going in Israel.
To the West Bank, I said. To a village of
 olives and almonds.
To see my people.

What kind of people? Arab people?

Uncles and aunts, grandmother, first and second
   cousins. Olive-gatherers.

Do you plan to speak with anyone? he said.
   His voice was harder
and harder, bitten between the teeth.

I wanted to say, No, I have come all this way
   for a silent reunion.
But he held my passport in his hands.
Yes, I said, We will talk a little bit. Families and
   weddings,
my father's preference in shoes, our grandmother's
   love for sweaters.
We will share steaming glasses of tea,
   the sweetness filling our throats.
Someone will laugh long and loosely,
so tears cloud my voice: O space of ocean waves,
how long you tumble between us, how little you
   dissolve!

We will eat cabbage rolls, rice with sugar and milk,
crisply sizzled eggplant. When the olives come
    sailing past
in their little white boat, we will line them
    on our plates
like punctuation. What do governments have to do
with such pleasure? Question mark.
YES I love you! Swooping exclamation.
Or the indelible thesis statement:
    it is with great dignity
we press you to our lips. 🦋

GARDENER appeared, waving his toothy rake.
Children with yellow bells in their hands
jumped the fence, snagging uniforms.
One boy trailed a purple vine.

They wouldn't be sorry,
pockets reeking jasmine,
mud staining shoes . . .
Who deserved flowers more?
Rich people who never came outside
or children stuck all day in school?

The sweaty gardener cursed them,
straightening branches.

Someone else lifted one large pink blossom
from the pavement beyond the fence,
found a scrap of tissue to wrap it in,
carried it home across the sea.

The dried petals lay on a table for months
whispering, *Where are we?*

Section Two

GASH of movement,
a spring of flight.

She saw them then
she did not see them.

The elegance of the gazelle
caught in her breath.

The next thing could have been weeping.

Rustic brown, a subtle spotted hue.

For years the Arab poets used "gazelle"
to signify grace,
but when faced with a meadow of leaping gazelle
there were no words.

Does one gazelle prefer another
of her kind?

They soared like history
above an empty page.

Nearby, giant tortoises
were kissing.

What else had we seen in our lives?
Nothing better than 19 varieties of gazelle
running free at the wildlife sanctuary . . .

"Don't bother to go there,"
said a man at our hotel.
"It's too far."

But we were on a small sandy island,
nothing was far!

We had hiked among stony ruins
to the Tree of Life.
We had photographed a sign that said
KEEP TO THE PATH in English and Arabic.

Where is the path?
Please tell me.
Does a gazelle have a path?
Is the whole air the path of the gazelle?

The sun was a hot hand on our heads.

Human beings have voices—
what have they done for us?

There is no gazelle
in today's headline.

The next thing could have been weeping . . .
Since when is a gazelle
wiser than people?

Gentle gazelle
dipping her head
into a pool of silver grass.

Bahrain

THE MAN with laughing eyes stopped smiling
to say, "Until you speak Arabic,
you will not understand pain."

Something to do with the back of the head,
an Arab carries sorrow in the back of the head
that only language cracks, the thrum of stones

weeping, grating hinge on an old metal gate.
"Once you know," he whispered, "you can
    enter the room
whenever you need to. Music you heard
    from a distance,

the slapped drum of a stranger's wedding,
wells up inside your skin, inside rain, a thousand
pulsing tongues. You are changed."

Outside, the snow had finally stopped.
In a land where snow rarely falls,
we had felt our days grow white and still.

I thought pain had no tongue. Or every tongue
at once, supreme translator, sieve. I admit my
shame. To live on the brink of Arabic, tugging

its rich threads without understanding
how to weave the rug . . . I have no gift.
The sound, but not the sense.

I kept looking over his shoulder for someone else
to talk to, recalling my dying friend
     who only scrawled
I can't write. What good would any grammar
     have been

to her then? I touched his arm, held it hard,
which sometimes you don't do in the Middle East,
and said, *I'll work on it*, feeling sad

for his good strict heart, but later in the slick street
hailed a taxi by shouting *Pain!* and it stopped
in every language and opened its doors. ✍

"Let's be the same wound if we must bleed.
Let's fight side by side, even if the enemy
is ourselves: I am yours, you are mine."
—Tommy Olofsson

'M NOT interested in
who suffered the most.
I'm interested in
people getting over it.

Once when my father was a boy
a stone hit him on the head.
Hair would never grow there.
Our fingers found the tender spot
and its riddle: the boy who has fallen
stands up. A bucket of pears
in his mother's doorway welcomes him home.
The pears are not crying.
Later his friend who threw the stone
says he was aiming at a bird.
And my father starts growing wings.

Each carries a tender spot:
something our lives forgot to give us.
A man builds a house and says,

"I am native now."
A woman speaks to a tree in place
of her son. And olives come.
A child's poem says,
"I don't like wars,
they end up with monuments."
He's painting a bird with wings
wide enough to cover two roofs at once.

Why are we so monumentally slow?
Soldiers stalk a pharmacy:
big guns, little pills.

If you tilt your head just slightly
it's ridiculous.

There's a place in this brain
where hate won't grow.
I touch its riddle: wind, and seeds.
Something pokes us as we sleep.

It's late but everything comes next. ✑

OVER BEDS wearing thick homespun cotton
   Sitti the Ageless floated
poking straight pins into sheets
   to line our fevered forms,
"the magic," we called it,
   her crumpling of syllables,
pitching them up and out,
   petals parched by sun,
the names of grace, hope,
   in her graveled grandmother tongue.
She stretched a single sound
   till it became two—
perhaps she could have said
   anything,
the word for peanuts,
   or waterfalls,
and made a prayer.

After telling the doctor "Go home,"
    she rubbed our legs,
pressing into my hand
    someone's lost basketball medal,
"Look at this man reaching for God."
    She who could not leave town
while her lemon tree held fruit,
    nor while it dreamed of fruit.
In a land of priests,
    patriarchs, muezzins,
a woman who couldn't read
    drew lines between our pain
and earth,
    stroked our skins
to make them cool,
    our limbs which had already
traveled far beyond her world,
    carrying the click of distances
in the smooth, untroubled soles
    of their shoes. 🍂

OU CAN'T be, says a Palestinian Christian
on the first feast day after Ramadan.
So, half-and-half and half-and-half.
He sells glass. He knows about broken bits,
chips. If you love Jesus you can't love
anyone else. Says he.

At his stall of blue pitchers on the Via Dolorosa,
he's sweeping. The rubbed stones
feel holy. Dusting of powdered sugar
across faces of date-stuffed *mamool*.

This morning we lit the slim white candles
which bend over at the waist by noon.
For once the priests weren't fighting
in the church for the best spots to stand.
As a boy, my father listened to them fight.
This is partly why he prays in no language
but his own. Why I press my lips
to every exception.

A woman opens a window—here and here
    and here—
placing a vase of blue flowers
on an orange cloth. I follow her.
She is making a soup from what she had left
in the bowl, the shriveled garlic and bent bean.
She is leaving nothing out. ❧

SHE SCRUBBED as hard as she could
with a stone.
Dipping the cloth, twisting the cloth.
She knew the cloth much better than most,
having stitched its vines of delicate birds.

The red, the blue, the purple beaks.
A tiny bird with head held high.
A second bird with fanning wings.
Her fingers felt the folded hem.

The water in her pan was cool.
She stood outside by the lemon tree.
Children chattered around her there.
She told the children, "Take care! Take care!"

What would she think of the world today?
She died when she was one hundred and six.
So many stains would never come out.
She stared at the sky, the darkening rim.

She called to the children, "Come in! Come in!"
She stood on the roof, tears on her face.
What was the thing she never gave up?
The simple love of her difficult place.

SERUM OF steam rising from the cup,
what comfort to be known personally by *Barbara*,
her perfect pouring hand and starched ascot,
known as the two easy eggs and the single pancake,
without saying.
What pleasure for an immigrant—
anything without saying.

My uncle slid into his booth.
I cannot tell you—how I love this place.
He drained the water glass, noisily clinking his ice.
My uncle hailed from an iceless region.
He had definite ideas about water drinking.
I cannot tell you—all the time. But then he'd try.

My uncle wore a white shirt every day of his life.
He raised his hand against the roaring ocean
and the television full of lies.
He shook his head back and forth
from one country to the other
and his ticket grew longer.

Immigrants had double and nothing all at once.
Immigrants drove the taxis, sold
    the beer and Cokes.
When he found one note that rang true,
he sang it over and over inside.
Coffee, honey.
His eyes roamed the couples
    at other booths,
their loose banter and casual clothes.
But he never became them.

Uncle who finally left in a bravado moment
after 23 years, *to live in the old country forever,*
to stay and never come back,
maybe it would be peaceful now,
maybe for one minute,

I cannot tell you—how my heart has settled at last.
But he followed us to the sidewalk
saying, *Take care, Take care,*
as if he could not stand to leave us.

I cannot tell—

how we felt
to learn that the week he arrived,
he died. Or how it is now,
driving his parched streets,
feeling the booth beneath us as we order,
oh, anything, because if we don't,
nothing will come. ✐

"What is it that is wrecking our lives?"
—Daud Kamal

HE BOY who ate poisoned fish in Sri Lanka
  covers his eyes.
Each time the plane shudders, his knuckles whiten.
He wants to be home.

Below us the hungry Atlantic pushes and pulls
its waves across the earth.
All we want is to land safely again,

we who calculate our luckiness, who worry
that the pocket must be growing a hole.
The bread seller of Aleppo
wanted only to sell his bread. And the Saudi women

who said, "Tell them we *are* oppressed, but *not* stupid,"
had just that message in mind.
We signed each others' notebooks as if

those addresses were a definite shore.
Once on a bus out of Nepal
I prayed for nothing but flat land.

It seemed so easy, being reduced
to a single wish! In those moments
I think our lives are laughing at us.

They know the moment a wish is answered
our hearts will open like sieves
and everything fall through again.

They know that women and men have been
wanting so much for so long
a flat highway will only remind us of heat,

of sleeping, the deliberate stones
crossing this season, the arrogant river
tumbling beneath. ✆

SKIN REMEMBERS how long the years grow
when skin is not touched, a gray tunnel
of singleness, feather lost from the tail
of a bird, swirling onto a step,
swept away by someone who never saw
it was a feather. Skin ate, walked,
slept by itself, knew how to raise a
see-you-later hand. But skin felt
it was never seen, never known as
a land on the map, nose like a city,
hip like a city, gleaming dome of the mosque
and the hundred corridors of cinnamon and rope.

Skin had hope, that's what skin does.
Heals over the scarred place, makes a road.
Love means you breathe in two countries.
And skin remembers—silk, spiny grass,
deep in the pocket that is skin's secret own.
Even now, when skin is not alone,
it remembers being alone and thanks something
    larger
that there are travelers, that people go places
larger than themselves.   ✍

EVEN ON a sorrowing day
the little white cups without handles
would appear
filled with steaming hot tea
in a circle on the tray,
and whatever we were able
to say or not say,
the tray would be passed,
we would sip
in silence,
it was another way
lips could be speaking together,
opening on the hot rim,
swallowing in unison.

LOVE odd collections:
buttons, lightbulbs, toothpaste tubes.
The man who gathered sugar packets for 37 years.
So when I heard about the hats made from rinds of
     lemons & limes
a century ago, decorated with bits of frill & cloth
to represent the tribes & occupations of the time,
I loved William Yale, this strange gift for his
     Jerusalem bride.
I sent my Boston friends to see the hats.
They got lost driving to the exhibition in a
     rainstorm,
more lost coming home.
But they reported the hats made by children's hands
lined up teeny tiny, displayed on thimbles & walnuts,
were withered only a bit around the edges
as any rind might be after so long.
And they felt hypnotized!

A sudden tangy hopefulness
rose up from the hats,
a stunning wish for women & men
with tinier heads
to solve Jerusalem's troubles. ✺

OUTSIDE
tuned in to the night-blooming cereus
Channel 1 a.m.

Creamy petals
halfway open
striking white
when a crack of thunder
split the sky
ruffling branches
gust of cold

It was winter in a minute
O I could miss who said what said
but catch the coming of winter
let me be there
please

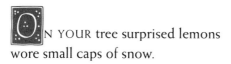

For Mona Saudi

STAYING CLOSE

ON YOUR tree surprised lemons
wore small caps of snow.

The bowl of steaming lentils
opened its wide mouth as we sat and sat,
stitching the seam of talk,
till the man with the rug from Baghdad arrived
rolling out its long length inside your door.

It was orange. It looked happy.
He had just come overland with a bundle of rugs.

When you kissed him good-bye on both cheeks
I wanted to kiss him too,
not for our offhand greeting,
or his deep eyes like furry animals
curled into lairs for the winter,
but for each doorway in Baghdad
with a rug in front of it
and humans moving in and out.

"We thought of ourselves as people of culture.
How long will it be till others see us that way again?"
—Iraqi friend

IN HER first home each book
had a light around it.
The voices of distant countries
floated in through open windows,
entering her soup and her mirror.
They slept with her in the same thick bed.

Someday she would go there.
Her voice, among all those voices.
In Iraq a book never had one owner—it had ten.
Lucky books, to be held often
and gently, by so many hands.

Later in American libraries she felt sad
for books no one ever checked out.

She lived in a country house beside a pond
and kept ducks, two male, one female.
She worried over the difficult relations
of triangles. One of the ducks
often seemed depressed.
But not the same one.

During the war between her two countries
she watched the ducks more than usual.
She stayed quiet with the ducks.
Some days they huddled among reeds
or floated together.

She could not call her family in Basra
which had grown farther away than ever
nor could they call her. For nearly a year
she would not know who was alive,
who was dead.

The ducks were building a nest.   ✍

o thin, it fits anywhere
without making a lump.
Onion skin.
Pocket-size, slips right in.
With a little bendable black cover
to look dressed up.

He's riffling the pages
looking for our lost cousin in Alaska.
We don't even know
his first name.
Smudged phone number,
half-disappeared.
We don't know if he's in a town
or on the tundra.

Why would I call him?

My cousin pours his deep eyes
into mine.
In our family we laugh and cry
like two bites of the same dessert.

Maybe he has something to tell us.
Maybe he doesn't know our news.

Honey gimme that book.
Look, it's transclucent.
I can hold it up to the lamp
and see the bulb.
Didn't you meet anyone
in the last 20 years? ✍

SHE SCRABBLES deep into loam and leaves
digging with turtle claws
to make a cavity just her size.
Pressing eyes and mouth
down into cool,
over by the fence,
on a strip of land where nobody walks,
what is she thinking?
Half shells of turtle eggs
scattered around the grass
all summer.

The turtle expert said,
She can't hear—
See these red streaks in place of ears?
Give her a pool—
She likes water more than land,
though obviously makes her way on land
when pressed—how long did you say you've had her?

But she turns her head when we approach
even from the rear.
She feels your footfall
on the earth.

Maybe we are stepping too heavily,
disturbing her air.
Red Slider slows us down,
we gather with strips of papaya, small knives.
On a ninety degree day
we tiptoe through her yard.

*

For years, I rarely slept well,
was always catching my breath,
maybe it wasn't just asthma,
maybe the far-away footfalls
jarring this close ground,
the running feet, pound of days,
dodging bullets, steps of the forgotten
trudging through rubble,
my cousins hiding in their houses,
Ibtisam's brother losing two kids in a minute,
the little blind Palestinian girls saying
"But we didn't cry!"
when their school was bombed,
no wonder we shudder and thrash,

a lack of oxygen in the news,
water tipping in the pool
to drown half its people, regular people
scrambling for a refuge,
for a cool place in the leaves,
if they had any leaves,
if their trees weren't uprooted
when they try to sleep,
curled in knots,
the earth rattling beneath them. ☍

"... under a siege imposed by the Israeli military
occupation. All movement of people and goods is
completely restricted and controlled by the Israeli
army. The army has dug trenches and moats and built
mounds of dirt to close Palestinian towns and villages ..."

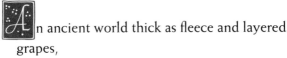n ancient world thick as fleece and layered
   grapes,
stones stacked into walls on hillsides,
the neat lineage of orchards . . .
even now in shuttered rooms
silver needles pulling thread till
a bird rises from the cloth
to fly in circles
over a scene she does not
recognize.

Where is her nesting place,
the safe slot between branches?

There is a language
between two languages
called Mean but who will admit
they are speaking it?

"Let's change places," the teenagers said.
"For a week, I'll be you and you be me."
Knowing if they did, they could never fight again.

Listen to them.

HE COULD hear them off in the forest,
massive branches breaking:
You are no good, will never be any good.

Sometimes they followed him,
rubbing out his tracks.
They wanted him to get lost
in the world of trees,
stand silently forever, holding up his hands.

At night he watched
the street lamp's light
soaking into his lawn.
He could bathe in its cool voice,
roll over to a whole different view.
What made them think
the world's room was so small?

On the table he laid out his clothes,
arranging the cuffs.
What he said to his enemies
was a window pushed high as it would go.
Come in, look for me where you think
I am. Then when you see no one is there,
we can talk. ✍

1.

PEOPLE PASS you in the street
and do not see you.

Apparition, hidden river,
inhabitant of cracks . . .

After battering talk
a room clears
and you're on the ceiling
extending your silent hand
water of light
poured freely . . .

a hand, not a flag.
You don't believe in flags anymore.
You're not even sure
you believe in men.

Birds, children, silver trays—
no problem here.
Each day they trade their air
and song. They feed you.

2.

Rounding the last old city corner to school,
for years and years
a boy touched his finger to
the same chipped stone in a wall.

Befriending one another
was no trouble.

The boy knew what came next:
tight desk, stretching hours.

Sixty years later in another country
he tells one person about the stone.

Then goes outside
to stare into trees.

Is it still there?
He will find it.
What if it is not there?
He will find it.

S LONG as a mirror opening its eye
to stretch a room lengthwise

As long as the slow crawl of loosening paint
and the bending of slim wax tapers

As long as blue thread spinning
a vine of birds up one seam down the other
and the bodice don't forget the bodice
doubly thick with wings and hidden treasure

As long as my Sitti twists her hanky
around two small gold coins
in the bed   in the bed
and says she is not tired

As long as the bed
and all the people who slept in it

As long as the splitting of almonds
the stirring of lentils
the scent of *marimea*
and the Universal Laundry

As long as the question—what if I
were you?—has two heads

As long as the back of the skull is
vulnerable and the temple and the chest

As long as anyone feels exempt
or better and one pain is separate
from another and people are pressed flat
in any place

And longer

If every day the soldier slaps
another cousin's face ✍

N APPLE on the table

hides its seeds

so neatly

under seamless skin.

But we talk and talk and talk

to let somebody

in.

MY GRANDMOTHER is dead
but her green trunk
must still be sitting.
Sitting in the stone room
with an arch
and a single window.
Sitting in the cool light
that touches
the chipped lid.
And I wonder where the key has gone.
The key that lived
between her breasts
whether she slept or woke.
And wouldn't let anybody touch.
I wonder if they have
emptied the trunk
or left her squares of velvet
carefully folded,
her chips of plates,
the scraps and rubble she saved
and wouldn't let us see.
Wouldn't let us see
because every life
needs a hidden place.

And I pray they
have not emptied it.

We brought her rosy soap
for the hidden place.
Heavy wedge of chocolate
twisted in foil.
She tried to eat the foil.
We brought her nothing big enough
but she saved it all.
The uncle made fun of her.
She lived too long.
The Queen of Palestine.
She would turn her face away
when he said that.
He died first.

And we never stayed.
No we never stayed.
The trunk stayed.
The grapes shriveled in the village
and didn't come again.
This was a sadness beyond telling.
Maybe if they didn't mention it
the grapes would return.

The clay they used for jugs
also went away.
The young men
went away.
It was a hard place to be
if you were staying.

Why do I think of that key
still planted firmly in the crack
over her heart?
She used to say the stone
was smarter than people
because it never went away.

HOLY LAND EXPERIENCES BIGGEST SNOWFALL
IN 50 YEARS

IF SOMEONE'S lemon tree
disappears under a drift

If your auto with the blue license plates
your goat or my aged donkey
If the clay jar in which your mother
hauled water for sixty years

If the snow piles up past everyone's windows
all of the windows

PALESTINIANS & ISRAELIS WORKED TOGETHER
IN THE WEST BANK TO RESCUE . . .

a sweeter sentence than *baklava*

than all the oranges of Jericho
offered up to God!

TOP ISRAELI OFFICIAL HINTS AT
"SHARED" JERUSALEM

After all this time, just a hint?
He could sing it loudly.
Chant from the top of a wall.

He's a top official, after all.
Why whisper?
Why not stand in the street

bursting with syllables
shocking taxi drivers and bread sellers—
Why not, why not, why not?

Does a mother hint that she loves her child?

Now, while we are fresh.
While the century is still a wide-open page.
Now, a new story to be made
and everyone, with their fragrant nouns

and muscular verbs
to write it.

MR. DAJANI, calling from Jericho,
wants to talk about books.
It is not always easy to get books there
in such an ancient city, such a low-lying city.
He ordered some—they did not come.
In the background, a great melodious squawking,
Mr. Dajani's voice muffled by din.
Is he living with parrots?
"No, I have swans! Beautiful swans
waiting for you to visit them!
We have chickens with babies,
we have many eggs!"

Is he a teacher?
"No, I am the weatherman of Jericho!"
Doesn't Jericho always have the
    same steamy weather?
If we came to Jericho and said his name,
anyone would lead us to him,
the swans would call us home.

"Madame, we've been having a bit of trouble
    over here."
Is he the king of understatement too?
"So I am writing a paper.

Trying to write a paper, trying my best.
Remember when you said 'cousins, not enemies'—
I agree with that, but it's a little hard to hold on to
    these days.
Could you write me a letter, say more?
I want it to be possible."

Who could resist this man?
I mail him books,
a fat packet of pages
written in the middle of the night.
He leaves phone messages,
omitting crucial digits in his number.
The swans are on my message machine.

On the day of the worst news yet, he calls again.
"Hey, they are bombing us now
    with American planes.
But the books came! I want you to know
we never stop holding our branch of the olive tree
even though for some it is such a little branch.
All we ever wanted was respect.
Regular bits of dignity and respect.
Too much to hope?
Here in the greenest city in the world,

flowers, lemons, watermelons, vegetables,
we need the roundtable and the peace of the talks.
We are not cheering for anybody dead.
Please remember us!
We'll be waiting you here, swans and I.
Books and papers,
connection between hearts.
We'll never cut the cord." ✑

July 2001

YOU CANNOT stitch the breath
back into this boy.

A brother and sister were playing with toys
when their room exploded.

*In what language
is this holy?*

The Jewish boys killed in the cave
were skipping school, having an adventure.

Asel Asleh, Palestinian, age 17, believed in the field
beyond right and wrong where people
    come together

to talk. He kneeled to help someone else
stand up before he was shot.

*If this is holy,
could we have some new religions please?*

Mohammed al-Durra huddled against his father
in the street, terrified. The whole world saw him die.

An Arab father on crutches burying his 4 month girl
   weeps,
"I spit in the face of this ugly world."

*

Most of us would take our children over land.
We would walk the fields forever homeless
with our children,
huddle under cliffs, eat crumbs and berries,
to keep our children.
This is what we say from a distance
because we can say whatever we want.

*

No one was right.
Everyone was wrong.
What if they'd get together
and say that?
At a certain point
the flawed narrator wins.

People made mistakes for decades.
Everyone hurt in similar ways
at different times.
Some picked up guns because guns were given.

If they were holy it was okay to use guns.
Some picked up stones because they had them.
They had millions of them.
They might have picked up turnip roots
or olive pits.
Picking up things to throw and shoot:
at the same time people were studying history,
going to school.

*

The curl of a baby's graceful ear.

The calm of a bucket
waiting for water.

Orchards of the old Arab men
who knew each tree.

Jewish and Arab women
standing silently together.

Generations of black.

Are people the only holy land?

"A TRUE Arab knows how to catch
a fly in his hands,"
my father would say. And he'd prove it,
cupping the buzzer instantly
while the host with the swatter stared.

In the spring our palms peeled.
True Arabs believed watermelon
could heal fifty ways.
I changed these to fit the occasion.

Years before, a girl knocked,
wanted to see the Arab.
I said we didn't have one.
After that, my father told more stories,
"Shihab"—"shooting star"—
a good name, borrowed from the sky.
Once I said, "When we die, we give it back?"
He said that's what a true Arab would say.

Today the headlines clot in my blood.
A Palestinian boy dangles a toy truck
on the front page.
Homeless fig, this tragedy with a terrible root
is too big for us. What flag can we wave?

I wave the flag of stone and seed,
table mat stitched in blue.

I call my father, we talk around the news.
It is too much for him,
neither of his two languages can reach it.
I drive into the country to find sheep, cows,
to plead with the air:
Who calls anyone *civilized*?
Where can the crying heart graze?
What does a true Arab do now?

Think of something you said. Now write
what you wish you had said.
—William Stafford

1.

I wish I had said nothing.
Had not returned the call.
Had left the call dangling, a shirt from one pin.

And settled into the deep pink streaks of sundown
without a single word flying from my mouth.
The thousand small birds of January

in their smooth soaring cloud
finding the trees.

2.

Or if I had to say something,
only a tiny tiny thing. A well-shaped phrase.
Smoothed off at the edges like a child's wooden
    cow.
That nobody would get a splinter from.

3.

No one has a deep wish to quote you accurately.
They want a good *story*.
It is not your story really, it is theirs.
So they do not care if they run the four sentences
    you said
(one that you really *said*, then three loose ones you
    answered
their chatty questions with)
into one sentence as if you said all that
together. Like a *speech*.
It sounds good to them.
They do not care
how it sounds to you.

4.

And you will have to live with it.
Foolishness ringing in your head.
Will not be able to sleep.
Nights on end. Nights standing on ends
like tops spun on pointy heads.
Will hate yourself for forgetting
this is what reporters do.
Will feel sudden sympathy for movie stars.
They do not care about you either.
But they have seen their words and silences defiled.
Will promise never again to answer questions
dashed across a phone line. Write it down.
Always write it down. Say it slowly. Say it
the way you learned words. Say it
as if words count.
One two. The shoe still has
a buckle. *☞*

ACKNOWLEDGMENTS

"The Small Vases from Hebron" previously appeared in *The Best American Poetry 1996*, edited by Adrienne Rich (Scribner, 1996).

Permission to reprint copyrighted material is gratefully acknowledged to the following:

BOA Editions, Ltd., for "Even at War," "The Grieving Ring," "For the 500th Dead Palestinian, Ibtisam Bozieh," "Those Whom We Do Not Know," "My Grandmother in the Stars," "Arabic," "Jerusalem," "Holy Land," from *Red Suitcase* by Naomi Shihab Nye. Copyright © 1994 by Naomi Shihab Nye. And for "Steps," "The Palestinians Have Given Up Parties," "The Small Vases from Hebron," "Darling," "Fundamentalism," "Half-and-Half," "My Uncle's Favorite Coffee Shop," "Ducks", from *Fuel* by Naomi Shihab Nye. Copyright © 1998 by Naomi Shihab Nye. Reprinted with the permission of BOA Editions, Ltd.

Far Corner Books for "Different Ways to Pray," "My Father and the Figtree," "Biography of an Armenian Schoolgirl," "The Words Under the Words," "Spark" (originally "Jerusalem"), "The Man Who Makes Brooms," "The Garden of Abu Mahmoud," "For Mohammed on the Mountain," "Lunch in Nablus City Park," "Arabic Coffee," "Two Countries," "What He Said to His Enemies," "Blood," from *Words Under the Words: Selected Poems* by Naomi Shihab Nye. Copyright © 1995 by Naomi Shihab Nye. Reprinted by permission of Far Corner Books, Portland, Oregon. Special thanks to Tom Booth.